Remember When...?

Remember Ziggy Stardust and bellbottomed jeans?
How about Soul Train, or All in the Family?
Can you remember when streaking was common,
or when Evel Knievel was uncommonly cool?

Then you must be ready for a 70s party!

THIS BOOK OF MEMORIES PRESENTED TO:

_____

ON THE OCCASION OF:

_____

DATE:

1970

- The first Earth Day is celebrated
- Jimi Hendrix and Janis Joplin, dead (at age 27) within weeks of each other
- The Environmental Protection Agency is created by Richard Nixon's administration
- Garry Trudeau's comic strip *Doonesbury* debuts.

1974

- Richard Nixon resigns the presidency and is subsequently pardoned by Gerald R. Ford
- Mikhail Baryshnikov defects to the United States
- Karen Silkwood dies in a mysterious car crash en route to meet with union officials and a reporter

1971

- Disney World opens in Florida
- The voting age is lowered to 18 by the 26th Amendment
- D.B. Cooper parachutes from a plane with $200,000, never to be seen again
- Prisoners riot and take hostages at Attica State Correctional Facility in New York state

1975

- Bill Gates and Paul Allen start Microsoft in an apartment in Albuquerque, New Mexico
- Former Teamsters Union president Jimmy Hoffa disappears
- Lynnette "Squeaky" Fromme tries to shoot President Ford

1972

- All cigarette advertising is banned from TV
- Laszlo Toth attacks Michelangelo's Pietà in the Vatican

1973

- In the Roe vs. Wade decision, the US Supreme Court legalizes abortion
- Congress passes the Endangered Species Act, and work on the Tellico Dam in Tennessee is halted to protect the snail darter fish
- The last American troops leave Vietnam
- The drought and subsequent famine in Ethiopia kills over 100,000
- OPEC cuts off oil shipments to the US and gas prices skyrocket

SETTING THE SCENE

1976

- Israel rescues a hijacked plane held by terrorists at Entebbe, Uganda
- An outbreak of a mysterious bacterial infection kills 34 at a Legionnaires convention
- The US celebrates its Bicentennial
- John Lennon receives his green card after years of wrangling with US Immigrations

1977

- Jimmy Carter takes office as the 39th president of the US, and within days pardons most Vietnam war draft dodgers
- New York City has a massive power blackout
- Elvis Presley dies at Graceland, age 42

AK-47
8-track tapes
apartheid
anti-war protests
black power   Anita Bryant
consciousness-raising
Jonestown   the draft
the Equal Rights Amendment
smiley face   Have a nice day!
hostage crisis   Doonesbury
Evel Knievel   Howard Hughes
George Lucas   Linda Lovelace
peanut farmer
reverse discrimination

THE BUZZ

Age of Aquarius
Inflation   DMZ
the Me Decade   Phyllis Schlafly
the Troubles
the silent majority
The Washington Post
Gloria Steinem   skateboards
streaking   tall ships
women's lib

1978

- *Hustler* publisher Larry Flynt is shot and paralyzed from the waist down outside a Georgia courthouse
- *Star Wars* rules the box office
- Cult leader Jim Jones and his followers commit mass suicide in Guyana, South America

1979

- A near melt-down occurs at the Three Mile Island nuclear power plant in Pennsylvania
- Mother Teresa receives the Nobel Peace Prize

TOP OF THE CHARTS

★**Bridge Over Troubled Water** (Simon & Garfunkel)

★**Let It Be** (The Beatles)

★**I'll Be There** (Jackson 5)

★**Close to You** (The Carpenters)

★**Stairway to Heaven** (Led Zeppelin)

★**Free Bird** (Lynyrd Skynyrd)

★**What's Goin' On** (Marvin Gaye)

★**Kiss an Angel Good Morning** (Charley Pride)

★**American Pie** (Don McLean)

★**Theme from Shaft** (Isaac Hayes)

★**I Am Woman** (Helen Reddy)

★**The First Time Ever I Saw Your Face** (Roberta Flack)

★**Crocodile Rock** (Elton John)

★**Tie a Yellow Ribbon Round the Ole Oak Tree** (Tony Orlando & Dawn)

★**The Way We Were** (Barbra Streisand)

★**I Honestly Love You** (Olivia Newton-John)

★**Rhinestone Cowboy** (Glen Campbell)

★**The Wreck of the Edmund Fitzgerald** (Gordon Lightfoot)

★**Love to Love You Baby** (Donna Summer)

★**Disco Duck Part 1** (Rick Dees)

★**Tonight's the Night** (Rod Stewart)

★**You Make Me Feel Like Dancing** (Leo Sayer)

★**Short People** (Randy Newman)

★**Roxanne** (The Police)

★**Just the Way You Are** (Billy Joel)

★**That's the Way (I Like It)** (HC & the Sunshine Band)

★**Love Will Keep Us Together** (Captain & Tennille)

★**My Sharona** (The Knack)

★**Superstition** (Stevie Wonder)

★**Joy to the World** (Three Dog Night)

★**Maggie May** (Rod Stewart)

★**American Woman** (Guess Who)

★**Lean On Me** (Bill Withers)

★**Close to You** (Carpenters)

arena rock

angel dust/fairy dust

Blues Brothers

Cheech & Chong

Concert for Bangladesh

Born to Run   disco

Dark Side of the Moon

Thick as a Brick

KISS

glam rock

Freddy Mercury

FM radio

glitter rock

Johnny Rotten

Casey Kasem

**Mad Dogs &
Englishmen**

THE BUZZ

Motown

New Wave

punk rock

Sid Vicious

southern rock

wah-wah pedal

Village People

Pop rock

Hotel California

Bernie Taupin   Sex Pistols
and Elton John

The Boogaloo

The Bump   **The Hustle**

Street Hustle

Latin Hustle

Night Fever line dance

The L.A. Hustle

The Robot   **The Lock**

The Bus Stop

CARE TO DANCE?

we loved our
television

Baretta
Mary Hartman, Mary Hartman
Barney Miller
Welcome Back, Kotter

Dallas
The Waltons

All in the Family
The Jeffersons

Hawaii Five-O
Happy Days   The Bob Newhart Show   Taxi

The Carol Burnett Show   Laverne & Shirley   **M*A*S*H**

Soap   **Charlie's Angels**   Saturday Night Live

The Mary Tyler Moore Show

Columbo   Mork & Mindy   The Flip Wilson Show

Streets of San Francisco   Soul Train

Starsky and Hutch The Dukes of Hazzard

Three's Company   Chico & the Man

The Rockford Files   Sanford and Son

Roots   The Partridge Family   Masterpiece Theatre   Kojak

The Odd Couple   Little House on the Prairie

MAUDE   **The Love Boat**

The David Frost Show   The Six Million Dollar Man

Wide World of Sports   **Mannix**

The Mike Douglas Show   Fernwood 2-Night

The Buzz

Slang

Allright!
Dig it
Bread Bummer Dude
Hip Cool Dy-no-mite
Acid flashback Boss Far out For real
Sock it to me laid back Cat
good (or bad) vibes Foxy What a trip!
Groovy Get Down Peace
Hang 10 Right on! Verrrry interesting
straight Trippin' Wow Hang loose
You bet your bippy Mellow out
May the Force be with you It's my bag
In the groove Outta sight!
uptight do your own thing
Let it all hang out Man

Freddie Prinz
Chevy Chase
Johnny Carson
Geraldine & Killer
Alex Haley
Woody Allen
Coneheads
Norman Lear
Lance Loud
nighttime soaps
Richard Pryor SNL
Not-Ready-for-
Prime-Time Players

MOVIES WE HAD TO SEE

- Alien
- All the President's Men
- American Graffiti
- The China Syndrome
- Chinatown
- A Clockwork Orange
- Close Encounters of the Third Kind
- Dirty Harry
- Dog Day Afternoon
- The Exorcist
- Grease
- Jaws
- The Last Picture Show
- Last Tango in Paris
- Love Story

- Norma Rae
- The Poseidon Adventure
- Saturday Night Fever
- Serpico
- Shaft
- Star Wars
- Superman
- The Towering Inferno
- The Sting
- Deliverance
- Apocalypse Now
- Blazing Saddles
- Five Easy Pieces
- 10
- Coming Home
- Cabaret

- Fiddler on the Roof
- The Goodbye Girl
- Women in Love
- Superfly
- A Touch of Class
- Alice Doesn't Live Here Anymore
- The Odessa File
- Paper Moon
- Papillon
- Save the Tiger
- The Rose
- Klute
- Monty Python's Life of Brian
- Network
- Harry and Tonto

THE BUZZ

Princess Leia

Blaxpolitation

Tubular Bells

Gonzo journalism

light saber

John Williams

Wookie

You talkin'
to me?

Roman Polanski

People
magazine

Academy Award® Best Pictures

1970 ....Patton	**1975** ....One Flew Over the Cuckoo's Nest
1971 ....The French Connection	**1976** ....Rocky
1972 ....The Godfather	**1977** ....Annie Hall
1973 ....The Sting	**1978** ....The Deer Hunter
1974 ....The Godfather Part II	**1979** ....Kramer vs. Kramer

On Broadway

A CHORUS LINE

COMPANY

THE ELEPHANT MAN

CHILDREN OF A LESSER GOD

BARNUM

FOLLIES

A LITTLE NIGHT MUSIC

SWEENEY TODD

OH! CALCUTTA!

GREASE

ANNIE

PIPPIN

SAME TIME, NEXT YEAR

EVITA

THE BEST LITTLE
WHOREHOUSE IN TEXAS

THE WIZ

DANCIN'

DEATHTRAP

SLEUTH

NO, NO, NANETTE

THE PRISONER
OF SECOND AVENUE

TWO GENTLEMEN OF VERONA

THAT CHAMPIONSHIP SEASON

RAISIN

THE RIVER NIGER

EQUUS

DA

AIN'T MISBEHAVIN'

ON THE TWENTIETH CENTURY

CHAPTER TWO

THE SHADOW BOX

THE ROBBER BRIDEGROOM

THE BELLE OF AMHERST

STICKS AND BONES

TRAVESTIES

on the Bookshelf

CULTURE

1970s

Where Were You ☆

1970
- The National Guard kills four students protesting the war at Kent State
- The US intensifies the bombing of Hanoi, and troops enter Cambodia

1971
- The March on Washington to protest the Vietnam War draws over 500,000
- The US Supreme Court upholds the constitutionality of school busing
- Daniel Ellsberg is arrested for leaking the Pentagon Papers to the *New York Times*

1972
- George McGovern is the Democratic candidate for president; Richard M. Nixon is re-elected in a landslide victory
- Bob Woodward and Carl Bernstein, writing for the *Washington Post*, expose corruption in the White House
- Nixon becomes the first US president to visit China
- A bungled burglary at the Democratic Party's national headquarters becomes a scandal known as Watergate

1973
- Televised hearings on Watergate begin, investigating a possible White House connection
- A Vietnam War cease-fire is signed in Paris, and US troops begin withdrawing from South Vietnam
- The American Indian Movement takes a stand against the US government in a siege at Wounded Knee
- Egypt and Syria open a surprise attack on Israel in what becomes known as the Yom Kippur War

1974
- Patty Hearst is kidnapped from her home by the SLA, a radical militant group
- A 55-mph speed limit becomes the law of the land
- Federal Election Campaign Act is signed into law, requiring full disclosure of all campaign contributions

1975
- The Freedom of Information Act is signed into law by President Ford
- Civil War breaks out in Angola
- The US Embassy in Saigon is evacuated as South Vietnam surrenders to North Vietnam

When... ?

1976

- The Supreme Court rules that busing is a legitimate option in desegregating the Boston School System
- Violence in Soweto Township, South Africa, opens the struggle to end apartheid
- Women are admitted to the US Army, Navy, and Air Force academies for the first time in history

1977

- The Panama Canal Treaty is signed
- Anwar Sadat is the first middle eastern leader to visit Israel since its establishment in 1948

1978

- Jimmy Carter brings Anwar Sadat and Menachim Began together at Camp David
- The Love Canal residential area is declared a disaster zone due to contamination from toxic waste
- The worst oil spill in history unfolds as the Amoco Cadiz sinks in waters off France

1979

- The US Embassy in Teheran is overrun by students; the hostages taken are held for 444 days
- Soviet forces invade Afghanistan

THE BUZZ

POW-MIA

ANGELA DAVIS

AGENT ORANGE

BOAT PEOPLE

DEEP THROAT

OIL EMBARGO   DESEGREGATION

DIRTY TRICKS
              MORAL MAJORITY

ENERGY CRISIS

FALL OF SAIGON   I AM NOT A CROOK!

KILLING FIELDS

INDOCHINA

KHMER ROUGE

MAYAGUEZ INCIDENT

OVAL OFFICE TAPES / 18 MIN.

POLITICAL
ENEMIES LIST

SANDANISTAS

SHUTTLE DIPLOMACY

TRICKY DICK

IDI AMIN

What We Wore

midi skirts
pastel tuxedos
caftans
Army surplus
boots
tube tops
cowboy boots
Afros
cords
platform shoes
granny dresses
bomber jackets
mini skirts
MooD rinGs
clogs
LEisurE suits
flares
floppy hats
silver-and-turquoise
denim jackets
gauchos
wide lapels
BellBottoms
plaid suits
ruffles on tux shirts
the Farrah Fawcett hair-do
long hair
Zapata moustache
satin jackets
designer jeans
ponchos
fringed jackets
shawl collars
lip gloss
polyester
low-riding jeans and slacks
pantsuits
for women
Nehru Jackets
the Annie Hall look
leather pants

The Buzz

- Palimony
- **quality time**
- "I'd like to teach the world to sing"
- "Nothing comes between me and my Calvins"
- **Primal scream therapy**
- androgyny
- CB radios (10-4 good buddy!)
- **Dungeons & Dragons**
- harvest gold

- space age design
- sexual revolution
- sting ray bikes
- designer labels
- **Pierre Cardin**

- Personal trainer
- **sportswear**
- threads
- Rolling Stone
- avocado green
- **Frito bandito**
- freaks / straights

- **Pet rock**
- Rolfing
- the mall
- **punk**
- roller rink
- studio 54
- **est**
- pull tabs

WHEELS
CHEVROLET CAMARO
PONTIAC GTO   AMC GREMLIN
CUSTOM VANS WITH AIR-BRUSHED MURALS
DATSUN Z
SUBARU BRAT

yogurt

health food   Crock pots

Adelle Davis   Juice bars   Granola

Vitamin C   quiche   Cool Whip®

Organic food   Hamburger Helper®

Brown rice   sloppy joes

                        tater tots

Pop Tarts®   Tab®   Fettuccine Alfredo

                              Rice-a-Roni®

Chex® party mix (homemade)

                                                            fondue

bundt cake   Frozen pizza   Buc Wheats® cereal

Fritos® corn chips   Jello® 1-2-3

        Pixie Stix®   Fruit striped gum

Kentucky Fried Chicken®

        Slurpees®   Manwich®

FOOD
TRENDS

Quiche

1 unbaked 9-inch pie shell
6 slices bacon, cooked and crumbled
1/2 onion, finely choped
2 c. shredded Swiss cheese
3 eggs, lightly beaten
1 1/2 c. half-n-half
1/2 tsp. salt
1/8 tsp. pepper
1 T. butter

Place crumbled bacon in pie shell, then sprinkle
in cheese and onion. In bowl, beat together eggs,
half-and-half, salt and pepper. Pour into pie shell.
Break cold butter into small pieces over top.
Bake in 375 oven 35-40 minutes or until a knife
inserted near the center comes out clean.
Allow to stand 10 minutes before serving. Serves 6.

THE WORLD SERIES

1970 ....Baltimore Orioles 4, Cincinnati Reds 1

1971 ....Pittsburgh Pirates 4, Baltimore Orioles 3

1972 ....Oakland Athletics 4, Cincinnati Reds 3

1973 ....Oakland Athletics 4, New York Mets 3

1974 ....Oakland Athletics 4, Los Angeles Dodgers 1

1975 ....Cincinnati Reds 4, Boston Red Sox 3

1976 ....Cincinnati Reds 4, New York Yankees 0

1977 ....New York Yankees 4, Los Angeles Dodgers 2

1978 ....New York Yankees 4, Los Angeles Dodgers 2

1979 ....Pittsburgh Pirates 4, Baltimore Orioles 3

THE STANLEY CUP

1970 ....Boston Bruins 4, St. Louis Blues 0

1971...........Montreal Canadiens 4, Chicago Blackhawks 3

1972..........................Boston Bruins 4, New York Rangers 2

1973...........Montreal Canadiens 4, Chicago Blackhawks 2

1974..........................Philadelphia Flyers 4, Boston Bruins 2

1975 ....Philadelphia Flyers 4, Buffalo Sabres 2

1976................Montreal Canadiens 4, Philadelphia Flyers 0

1977 ....Montreal Canadiens 4, Boston Bruins 0

1978 ....Montreal Canadiens 4, Boston Bruins 2

1979..................Montreal Canadiens 4, New York Rangers 1

THE NBA CHAMPIONSHIP

1970
New York Knicks 4
Los Angeles Lakers 3

1971
Milwaukee Bucks 4
Baltimore Bullets 0

1972
Los Angeles Lakers 4
New York Knicks 1

1973
New York Knicks 4
Los Angeles Lakers 1

1974
Boston Celtics 4
Milwaukee Bucks 3

1975
Golden State Warriors 4
Washington Bullets 0

1976
Boston Celtics 4 Phoenix
Suns 2

1977
Portland Trail Blazers 4
Philadelphia 76ers 2

1978
Washington Bullets 4
Seattle Super Sonics 3

1979
Seattle Super Sonics 4
Washington Bullets 1

WHO WON? THE SUPERBOWL

THE BUZZ

Pelé

Roberto Clemente

Brooks Robinson

Rollie Fingers   Reggie Jackson

Bucky Dent

Johnny Bench

Charlie Hustle   Slam dunk

Skyhook

free agent

Bill Shoemaker

The Golden Bear

Terry Bradshaw

Leon Spinks

Franco Harris   Dr. J   Bruce Jenner

Roger Staubach

Bjorn Borg

Mark Spitz

Catfish Hunter   Martina Navratilova

George Steinbrenner

Bowie Kuhn

Olga Korbut   Chris Evert

Mr. October

jogging

Walter Payton

Bobby Orr

roller derby

SPORTS

1970s

18

A DECADE OF SPORTS

1970
- South Africa is banned from Olympic competition
- *Monday Night Football* premieres on ABC with Keith Jackson, Don Meredith, and Howard Cosell

1971
- Cassius Clay (now Muhammed Ali) is cleared of his draft-dodging conviction
- Stan Smith and Billie Jean King capture US Open tennis titles
- Jack Nicklaus is the first pro to win all four majors: the Masters, US Open, British Open and PGA Championship

1972
- Bobby Fischer becomes the first American World Chess Master by defeating Boris Spassky
- Winter Olympics are held in Sapporo, Japan, and the Summer Olympics are in Munich, West Germany
- US swimmer Mark Spitz wins seven gold medals

1973
- The designated hitter is given a trial in the American League
- Secretariat claims the first Triple Crown since 1948
- Billie Jean King beats Bobby Riggs in a tennis exhibition "Battle of the Sexes"
- O.J. Simpson becomes the first running back to rush more than 2000 yards in a single season

1974
- Hank Aaron breaks Babe Ruth's home run record
- Richard Petty dominates stock car racing, winning the Daytona 500 and the NASCAR Championship
- In the "Rumble in the Jungle," Muhammad Ali knocks out George Foreman

1975
- Arthur Ashe defeats Jimmy Connors at Wimbledon
- Ali defeats Frazier in the "Thrilla in Manila," a fight many regard as the greatest in boxing history

1976
- The NBA and ABA merge
- Winter Olympics are held in Innsbruck, Austria, where Dorothy Hamill wins a gold medal in figure skating
- Summer Olympics are held in Montreal, Canada, where Nadia Comaneci and Bruce Jenner are breakout stars
- Frank Robinson becomes pro baseball's first black manager

1977
- Extreme sportsman George Willig illegally climbs the south tower of the World Trade Center in less than four hours
- Swedish tennis star Bjorn Borg defeats Jimmy Connors at Wimbledon
- A.J. Foyt becomes the first driver to win the Indianapolis 500 four times
- Seattle Slew takes horse racing's Triple Crown

1978
- Muhammed Ali loses his title to Leon Spinks in a split decision in Las Vegas; later he reclaims his title from Spinks in New Orleans
- Affirmed is a Triple Crown winner, with Steve Cauthen up
- Jack Nicklaus is *Sports Illustrated*'s Sportsman of the Year

1975
- Michigan State wins the NCAA basketball championship against Indiana State, kicking off a long rivalry between Earvin "Magic" Johnson and Larry Bird
- St. Louis Cardinal Lou Brock steals his 935th base, becoming baseball's champion base-stealer to date

LIFE JUST WOULDN'T BE THE SAME WITHOUT...

- Apple® II
- Concorde's first flight
- facsimile machine
- Post-It® Notes
- telephone answering machines
- test-tube babies
- Xerox® photocopier

- VCRs (Betamax and VHS)
- Online ATMs
- Quartz wristwatch from Seiko®
- soft contact lenses
- Food processor
- Intel's® microprocessor
- computer chip

- Nike® running shoes
- HBO
- Atari's® Pong video game
- Disposable razors
- Call waiting
- MRI
- Sony® Walkman

lunar rover
Apollo 13
Louise Brown
continental drift
DDT   energy crisis
Werner Erhard (est)
Hare Krishnas
inflation
Steve Jobs and Steve Wozniak
Richard Leakey

'THE BUZZ

Mars landing
NASA
EPA   recession
Karen Ann Quinlan
Three Mile Island
Soyuz II

CHECKLIST FOR THE PERFECT PARTY

THREE WEEKS BEFORE:

- ☐ Plan the occasion > *a 70s nostalgia party*　　　　☐ Create a compatible guest list
- ☐ Choose a location that will accommodate the number of guests
- ☐ Send invitations [date, time (start/end), place, directions] > *Ask guests to dress in clothing of the era*
- ☐ Plan and select decorations > *This can include old yearbooks, record albums and other memorabilia*
- ☐ Begin collecting materials and creating props
  > *Visit garage sales for old 45s and LPs, even old clothes*　> *Movie memorabilia stores are good sources*
- ☐ Prepare menu and grocery list > *Consider using food from the era for extra nostalgia*
- ☐ Select and hire caterer/serving help (if using)

A FEW DAYS BEFORE:

- ☐ Call any guests who have not responded　　　　☐ Buy groceries and beverages
- ☐ Prepare and refrigerate/freeze food items that can be made in advance
- ☐ Make party costume or select outfit

ONE DAY BEFORE:

- ☐ Clean house, party room facility or other party site　　☐ Set up and arrange party room
- ☐ Thaw out frozen party foods　　　　　　　　　　　☐ Get out serving pieces
- ☐ Coordinate last-minute arrangements with caterer, servers (if using)

THE DAY OF:

- ☐ Decorate party room　　　　☐ Prepare and arrange remaining food
- ☐ Coordinate set-up, service, cleanup with hired helpers (if using)
- ☐ Mentally travel through party > *BEGINNING: arrivals and introductions*　> *MIDDLE: food and activities; have everyone sign the book*　> *END: wrap it up! Party favors, Polaroid photos*
- ☐ Dress in party outfit　　　　☐ Await guests
- ☐ Have a good time!

HAPPY DAY!

Hope You Enjoyed Your Party... We Sure Did!